T0262445

TINY DYNAMITE

Abi Morgan

TINY DYNAMITE

OBERON BOOKS
LONDON

WWW.OBERONBOOKS.COM

First published in 2001 by Oberon Books Ltd.
521 Caledonian Road, London N7 9RH
Tel: +44 (0) 20 7607 3637 / Fax: +44 (0) 20 7607 3629
e-mail: info@oberonbooks.com
www.oberonbooks.com

Reprinted with corrections 2003

Copyright © Abi Morgan 2001 & 2003

Abi Morgan is hereby identified as author of this play in
accordance with section 77 of the Copyright, Designs and Patents
Act 1988. The author has asserted her moral rights.

All rights whatsoever in this play are strictly reserved and applica-
tion for performance etc. should be made before commencement
of rehearsal to Independent Talent Group Ltd., Oxford House, 76
Oxford Street, London W1D 1BS. No performance may be given
unless a licence has been obtained, and no alterations may be
made in the title or the text of the play without the author's prior
written consent.

This book is sold subject to the condition that it shall not by way
of trade or otherwise be circulated without the publisher's consent
in any form of binding or cover or circulated electronically other
than that in which it is published and without a similar condition
including this condition being imposed on any subsequent
purchaser.

A catalogue record for this book is available from the British
Library.

ISBN: 978-1-84002-241-4

Cover design: Eureka! Design Consultants Ltd

Visit www.oberonbooks.com to read more about all our books
and to buy them. You will also find features, author interviews and
news of any author events, and you can sign up for e-newsletters
so that you're always first to hear about our new releases.

Tiny Dynamite was first performed at the Traverse Theatre, Edinburgh, on 3 August 2001, with the following cast:

Lucien	Scott Graham
Anthony	Steven Hoggett
Madeleine	Jasmine Hyde
Director	Vicky Featherstone
Co-directors	Scott Graham
	and Steven Hoggett
Designer	Julian Crouch
Lighting Designer	Natasha Chivers
Original Music and Sound	Nick Powell

Tiny Dynamite was remounted in February 2003 at the Lyric Theatre Studio, Hammersmith. The cast was as follows:

Lucien	Scott Graham
Anthony	Steven Hoggett
Madeleine	Lesley Hart
Production Photography	Manuel Harlan

With thanks to: Tom Morris, John McGrath and Fiona Gasper, Hetty Shand, Lyric Theatre

Characters

ANTHONY
early/mid 30's

LUCIEN
early/mid 30's

MADELEINE
early 20's

The play is set over one summer.

'I think everything has the potential to be lethal in context. A friend was living in a mobile home in Darwin during the infamous hurricane. He and his wife had to abandon their trailer and run for shelter in a nearby hotel. When they were holed up in the hotel with a lot of other people, they could hear all this thudding on the door, they didn't know if it was others trying to get in – they didn't open the door because the wind was too strong – and the next morning, when they opened the door, it was embedded with splinters and pieces of glass, pieces of straw. These normally benign things, fragile things, would've been lethal, if they had opened the door. That really stuck in my imagination, it was like that story about throwing a sandwich off the Empire State Building and cracking a paving stone – this idea of being killed by a sandwich. These ideas led to those pieces where I shot things through guns that weren't bullets, using things like pearls and money as ammunition.'

Cornelia Parker

A Roadstop

LUCIEN is sitting in his car.

LUCIEN: A shy boy is coming home one day through the city he grew up in when suddenly he gets caught in a terrible storm. Fearful of lightning and loud noises and bad things, the shy boy shelters as best he can, forks of lightning falling down hard around him, burning out street lights and sparking rain on Tarmac. His best friend, a small boy, the runt of the litter, scorns his terror, for nothing scares him.

ANTHONY runs on stage, carrying a bag of coffees, it's raining, he's sheltering as he runs towards –

The runt boy, a quirky child, always the wild card, is already betraying the early signs of mental disease. Above him rage the elements, all around him, striking buildings, and sending local shopkeepers scurrying, but the runt boy is fearless and taunts the sky. His best friend, the shy boy of nervous disposition, pleads with him to come and shelter. He warns if he is not careful he will lose his life.

LUCIEN looks up to see ANTHONY standing outside. LUCIEN winds down the window –

Suddenly accepting that this is the worst that can happen to him, the runt boy decides to see if death will come to him. The shy boy tells him to stop mucking around it's late. Standing in a central place the runt boy ignores him, holding out his arms, waiting for the lightning to strike him down.

ANTHONY is standing in the rain, looking up. He sees LUCIEN staring and turns hurrying to the car.

It does not. The runt boy walks home amazed at his own good fortune, scoffing the shy boy for his lack of courage.

As ANTHONY is about to climb into the car he notices:

Still laughing as he arrives outside his front door, the runt boy reaches up for the doorhandle.

ANTHONY slides down next to the LUCIEN, he hands him a coffee, LUCIEN takes drinks, reading the paper oblivious.

A rogue fork of lightning bounces off the letter box, catching the runt boy hard across the chest.

ANTHONY chinks his paper cup of coffee with LU-CIEN.

ANTHONY: Kapow!

LUCIEN does not even look up from reading.

LUCIEN: Kapow!

They both drink oblivious.

The runt boy falls down to the ground. He is six years old. A scorch mark visible across his chest.

LUCIEN finally looks up from his paper.

ANTHONY: What you reading?

LUCIEN: Back page.

ANTHONY: Still reading the freak fucking accidents?

LUCIEN: There's no such thing as a *freak* fucking accident.

LUCIEN drinks his coffee. A young girl, MADE-LEINE stands hitching on the other side of the road. ANTHONY stares as if momentarily recognising her. It is as if for one moment she is there and then she's gone. Beat.

ANTHONY: So are we going?

LUCIEN: Yeah, we're going.

Beat.

ANTHONY: So, let's go.

A car door slams. A crackle of electricity.

A House

A house, LUCIEN enters carrying a box; sound of bees buzzing, geese somewhere far off.

ANTHONY follows behind him, road map and luggage in hand.

LUCIEN: You don't have to carry –

ANTHONY: I can carry a fucking suitcase.

LUCIEN: …I can bring the luggage in.

ANTHONY takes in the room.

ANTHONY: It's nice.

LUCIEN: Yeah.

ANTHONY: There's a lake.

LUCIEN: Yeah.

ANTHONY: Where is this?

LUCIEN: It's far away. (*Beat.*) You take whichever room.

ANTHONY: You sure?

LUCIEN: Yeah, you take whichever room.

ANTHONY: This is great. There's a deck. We didn't have a deck last year.

LUCIEN: Glad you like it.

ANTHONY: The rent must be –

LUCIEN: No problem

ANTHONY: Great. Great. Light, it gets good light, makes you feel like you're outside, only inside.

LUCIEN: Anthony.

ANTHONY: (*Beat.*) Talking…talking too much.

Silence.

LUCIEN: I'll just go and get…

ANTHONY nods. LUCIEN goes to get more luggage from the car.

ANTHONY: Thanks for –

LUCIEN: …There's a bathroom. Why don't you go and –

ANTHONY nods.

ANTHONY: Do I stink?

LUCIEN nods. LUCIEN exits.

ANTHONY takes in the room. A bee buzzes around him. He doesn't move. He lets the bee buzz around him, quietly following its journey waiting until it lands in the palm of his hand.

As LUCIEN enters, he sees ANTHONY still hasn't moved.

LUCIEN: There should be towels.

ANTHONY: Right.

LUCIEN: Bathroom's probably through there. There should be a shower…a shower and a bath.

ANTHONY: Both? How clean do you want me? Lucien, this is –

LUCIEN: Good. Go and have a wash now.

ANTHONY nods, exits. LUCIEN waits, then goes to look through ANTHONY's bag. He opens it, looking in to find it empty as ANTHONY comes through, half undressed. LUCIEN stops. ANTHONY doesn't say anything. He opens his hand by the window, the sound of a bee buzzing returns as it flies away.

ANTHONY: Still had the bee in my hand.

LUCIEN nods. ANTHONY nods.

LUCIEN: It's not that I don't trust you.

ANTHONY: It's okay. I don't mind.

LUCIEN: I just thought –

ANTHONY: It's okay.

LUCIEN: We could go out for dinner later if you like

ANTHONY shrugs. ANTHONY exits. The return of the buzz of the bee. LUCIEN swats the bee away. The buzz carries through.

A Restaurant

LUCIEN and ANTHONY sit looking at their menus. Low level muzak. It's pretty empty.

LUCIEN: This is great.

ANTHONY: What you having?

LUCIEN: I don't know. You made up your mind yet?

ANTHONY: I might have the meat loaf.

LUCIEN: You normally –

ANTHONY: Yeah, I'm having the meat loaf.

LUCIEN: …The shellfish is the speciality. You normally have fish.

ANTHONY: Steak, I'll have steak.

LUCIEN: Surf and turf. (*Beat.*) You get fish with that.

ANTHONY: Fish and steak?

LUCIEN: That's what they do here.

ANTHONY: Nah, I won't have that. (*Beat.*) It's pretty empty.

LUCIEN: It's not in season yet, couple of weeks and –

ANTHONY: I know when the summer is. So how's work?

LUCIEN: Good. Busy.

ANTHONY: That's good. You been promoted yet?

LUCIEN: Yeah, February.

ANTHONY: That's great, Luce. (*Beat.*) Wicked.

LUCIEN: Sit in your chair, properly Anthony.

ANTHONY: Sorry… Sorry… Back's not high enough. Nice restaurant.

LUCIEN: It was recommended. In the paper, they do recommendations on the food pages.

ANTHONY: Yeah.

LUCIEN: Reviews and stuff.

ANTHONY: Yeah, I often read the paper. I try and read a paper least once a week.

LUCIEN: That's good. That great.

ANTHONY: Don't give me an Oscar for it.

LUCIEN: I didn't mean –

ANTHONY: (*Beat.*) I read it for the cartoons mainly.

LUCIEN: They're funny.

ANTHONY: I like them.

LUCIEN: Do you read fat dog and his –

ANTHONY: …Mrs…Yeah, yeah. I really like that one.

LUCIEN: I didn't know that. I never knew that. We'll buy you your own paper if you like.

ANTHONY: My *own* paper?

LUCIEN: While we're on holiday.

ANTHONY: *That's great.*

LUCIEN: I didn't mean –

ANTHONY: (*Beat.*) I know how to carry my own suitcase. I can navigate my way out of here.

LUCIEN: I'm not saying.

ANTHONY: Don't talk down to me. Don't creep around me. Don't try and be all smiles to me. I'm not stupid, you know I'm not stupid.

LUCIEN: Anthony

ANTHONY: I know what fucking surf and turf is.

Silence.

LUCIEN: I'm sorry.

ANTHONY: (*Beat.*) I'm sorry. (*Beat.*) Let's have a nice holiday.

ANTHONY nods. LUCIEN holds up his glass. They chink.

Kapow.

ANTHONY chinks glasses with him again.

Kapow, kapow.

The Deck

ANTHONY sits reading the newspaper on the steps, outside eating an early morning sandwich.

ANTHONY: A man is standing on the top of the Empire State Building. This is his first trip to America, a business trip on behalf of the small pharmaceutical company he works for in London England. The man is eating a sandwich delighted to be standing on top of New York's national monument looking out across a late morning skyline. He has calculated that he can finish eating his sandwich, spend a leisurely ten minutes in the gift shop buying his wife and small son an appropriate souvenir, take the lift down to the eleventh floor, descending the last ten flights of stairs and still have a good fifteen minutes to browse along the top shelf of the down town store next door and be in time for his first meeting of the day. He is proud that already he is using words like *store* instead of *shop*. He is almost a native. He looks at his watch, sees that he ought to be speeding up with his sandwich eating and then remembers that he has failed to alter his watch to cover the important time difference between the two countries; his own and America. Irritated, the man tosses the remainder of his sandwich over the side of the building, returning to his hotel for some extra hours sleep.

ANTHONY throws the tail-end of his sandwich away; a high long shot that sends the sandwich into oblivion.

A woman in the street below en route to her shift cleaning the bedrooms of an uptown hotel fails to see the sandwich falling from above. The sandwich which gathered weight with velocity struck the woman at a hundred and forty-eight mph, and cracked the paving stone below.

Slam of a van door. MADELEINE enters.

A verdict of accidental death was recorded. The sandwich was ham and egg.

Hum of bees, almost electricity.

A box of vegetables fall from above which are caught by the girl. The girl crosses the stage, carrying them.

MADELEINE: Excuse me. (*Silence.*) I brought your vegetables.

The crackle of the electricity above, ANTHONY looks up from reading then freezes on seeing her.

It's the pylon.

ANTHONY stares at her.

It's the sound of the electricity. It makes the lines vibrate. Creates a lot of static, in the atmosphere. People notice it.

ANTHONY stares at her. Silence.

Made you dream yet?

ANTHONY stares at her.

It doesn't effect everyone. (*Beat.*) Apples. You ordered apples and – (*She takes out a list and starts to read from it.*) …bananas. We couldn't get you French beans. It depends what's in season. We've put in broccoli instead.

ANTHONY: My friend does the ordering.

MADELEINE: It's the first time I've delivered to you. You've been here –

ANTHONY: Two weeks.

MADELEINE: Holiday?

ANTHONY: I've seen you –

MADELEINE: You're here on holiday?

ANTHONY: …hitching. You were hitching.

MADELEINE: Yeah. (*Beat.*) Maybe.

ANTHONY: I've seen you. (*Beat.*) I've seen you before.

Silence. ANTHONY keeps staring as MADELEINE slides the box down on the step.

MADELEINE: I need paying. (*Beat.*) Can you pay me?

ANTHONY: I don't have any money.

MADELEINE: Okay, that's fine. You can leave it till next week.

ANTHONY: You work at the restaurant. They do good steak. I didn't do the surf bit. My friend had lobster. It had good mayonnaise.

MADELEINE: Thanks.

ANTHONY: It's difficult to make. (*Beat.*) I hear. Mayonnaise.

MADELEINE: They buy it in big jars.

ANTHONY: Cheats.

MADELEINE: I don't eat there.

ANTHONY: I won't either now I know they're frauds. They really do that? They really really do that? It's disappointing. We're in the country. The land of home-made.

MADELEINE contemplates, makes to go.

My friend's the one who makes the money.

MADELEINE: Tell him he owes me –

ANTHONY: (*Offering apple.*) Do you want one?

MADELEINE: Nah, I can get them when I want. Perk of the job.

ANTHONY: How many jobs you got?

MADELEINE: Four.

ANTHONY: That's too many.

MADELEINE: Kills the time. I need the money.

ANTHONY: Four jobs is too much.

MADELEINE nods her goodbyes and makes to go.

You shouldn't hitch. (*He keeps staring at her.*) A girl shouldn't hitch. It could be dangerous.

MADELEINE: I do it all the time.

ANTHONY: You shouldn't. Anything could happen. Weirdos will pass and spy you and in their guises as friendly looking tourists and local shopkeepers, steal you away and chop you into pieces.

MADELEINE laughs.

MADELEINE: Tourists are never friendly. And the shop-keepers are never local. They come in from the city and sell tasteful shit –

ANTHONY: (*Beat.*) Don't you want the box back? (*Beat.*) What's your name?

MADELEINE takes the box from him, her hand grazes his. A long low hum, like the crackle of electricity, vibrating.

Static.

MADELEINE: Right. (*Beat.*) Must be the pylons.

ANTHONY stands up, goes to say something.

Madeleine.

LUCIEN enters, watching the scene:

ANTHONY: Anthony.

MADELEINE: And your mate's?

ANTHONY: (*Beat.*) The lobster.

MADELEINE laughs, makes to go. ANTHONY throws her an apple, she flicks one arm up, catches it without even looking.

(*Calling after.*) Madeleine. (*Beat.*) Nice. (*Beat.*) Have one anyway.

MADELEINE bites and exits. ANTHONY watches her as she goes.

The House

LUCIEN enters, carrying the bags of vegetables left on the deck.

LUCIEN: You lock the door, it's a simple thing to do. I left the bloody key there, hanging.

ANTHONY: I must have not noticed –

LUCIEN: Yeah.

ANTHONY: …I just got lost walking.

LUCIEN: You have to take some responsibility. You have to pull your weight.

ANTHONY: I will.

LUCIEN: It's a mess in here. You leave the door open, food out and things get in there. They make a mess and stuff. This is outside, this is not like a city –

ANTHONY: No, the fridge would have got mugged.

LUCIEN: Don't be funny. You trying to be funny?

ANTHONY just stares at him.

Don't do that thing… Don't. That stare thing.

ANTHONY: Someone comes in and moves the stuff.

LUCIEN: No Anthony.

ANTHONY: Ants can't move chairs.

LUCIEN: It's knocked over that's all.

ANTHONY: Furniture moves across the room. Tables
move right across the room. Big fucking ants that could
do
that –

LUCIEN: I reckon you do it. I reckon you do it in your
sleep.

ANTHONY: And it's not just today. It's not just if I leave
the door open.

LUCIEN: There are wild cats, they probably get in –

ANTHONY: No –

LUCIEN: Chairs don't move on their own. There's food
gone. Someone's eating the food at night.

ANTHONY: Exactly.

LUCIEN: You're eating the food at night.

ANTHONY: I eat during the day.

LUCIEN: I find stuff. I find jars open, cereal boxes ripped
apart.

ANTHONY: It isn't me. It isn't.

Silence.

LUCIEN: I don't care if it is. The way you live your life,
the way… You're not in circulation. It's not surprising
you forget these things. I leave the key by the door.

ANTHONY: I know how to do these things.

LUCIEN: When was the last time you locked up? When was the last time you even had a front door, Anthony?

ANTHONY: I'm grateful.

LUCIEN: Don't be grateful. Find a method. Find a series of buzzwords in your head that will give a bit of order to your day. Going out. Lock door. Key. By door. Lock. Exit. Enjoy.

ANTHONY: You pick me up. You pick me up and you bring me here and I know that, I appreciate that.

LUCIEN: You don't have to appreciate that. (*Beat.*) You just have to get well.

Silence.

ANTHONY: What's outside, Lucien?

LUCIEN: Trees. Wild cats. They won't harm you. The sound of water, the lake. That hum. Insects, lots of insects.

ANTHONY: I see shadows.

LUCIEN: It's just the trees.

ANTHONY: They cut across me at night, they wake me.

LUCIEN: You have a tree right outside your window.

ANTHONY: Shadows that find me in every corner.

LUCIEN: Sleep on the sofa. I don't mind, we can swap rooms if you like.

ANTHONY: Chairs don't move by themselves, Lucien.

LUCIEN: They're not moving.

ANTHONY: Tables don't fall over.

LUCIEN: They're right in the morning.

ANTHONY: You pick them up. You get up early and you pick them up. Am I right? (*Beat.*) I'm right. (*Silence.*) You know something Lucien, how long have we been doing this?

LUCIEN: What?

ANTHONY: This.

LUCIEN: A while. A long time.

Silence.

ANTHONY: And we never talk about her…

LUCIEN: (*Beat.*) Just get well, Anthony.

ANTHONY: You talk as if you don't want to see her again. As if she isn't –

LUCIEN: She isn't.

ANTHONY: We don't know that.

LUCIEN: If she's alive, Anthony, how does she come to you as a ghost?

ANTHONY: People can haunt you, dead or alive.

MADELEINE enters carrying a bunch of flowers.

Someone's coming for dinner.

LUCIEN does not dare to turn and look. ANTHONY stares at MADELEINE.

LUCIEN: Now you tell me.

ANTHONY: Luce.

LUCIEN: Yes.

ANTHONY: (*Beat.*) I think you'll like her.

> *MADELEINE holds out the flowers. LUCIEN reaches out to take them from her, as if seeing her for the first time.*

The House

ANTHONY is laying the table for supper, placing the fork down on the table. LUCIEN is pouring MADELEINE a drink. MADELEINE puts the flowers in a vase.

ANTHONY: I run really fast and then it touches me – Kapow! Right there on my – There…bounced from there to there – Kapow! Kapow! Like a fork, like a fork coming out the sky.

> *From above a fork comes flying down. ANTHONY catches it, without even looking.*

MADELEINE: You must have been…

LUCIEN: We were six –

ANTHONY: Nearly seven. And I'm standing there and it's raining. (*To LUCIEN.*) Wasn't it? It was really wet my boots. (*To LUCIEN.*) Weren't they?

LUCIEN: …They were overflowing –

ANTHONY: …overflowing with water. Which is danger-ous. Water and electricity you can see its –

MADELEINE: You're bacon. You are potentially bacon.

ANTHONY: Exactly. She gets this. Do you see this girl gets this? I'm standing there and I'm like, *Come on, hit me then*. And nothing, nothing, I don't get hit or nothing so shy boy here says –

LUCIEN: I wanted to, I wanted to get home.

ANTHONY: Shy boy's all moody and I'm running and laughing ahead of him, nothing's going to get me, so we get to my front door and –

MADELEINE: I know what you are going to say. I know what you're going to say.

ANTHONY: It's like the worst –

LUCIEN: It's like the worst place –

ANTHONY: The worst place I could be standing. Lightning, bam! On the front door and then, Kapow – I'm six and it hits me, Kapow on the chest just like that –

MADELEINE: Jesus.

Silence.

ANTHONY: It's funny.

Silence.

MADELEINE: Freaky.

ANTHONY: I had a scorch mark –

LUCIEN: It was a big mother of a scorch mark.

ANTHONY: Right across, didn't I?

LUCIEN: Yep.

ANTHONY: Right across my chest.

Silence. MADELEINE doesn't react.

MADELEINE: Amazing.

ANTHONY: Do you want, do you want some more to drink? (*Scooping up her glass.*) He thinks it was the rubber.

MADELEINE: I'm fine.

ANTHONY: I'll get you a top up. He swears it was the rubber in my boots. (*To LUCIEN.*) We've got another bottle?

LUCIEN nods.

MADELEINE: Must have been –

ANTHONY: A miracle. (*To LUCIEN.*) Wasn't it?

LUCIEN: Definitely touched.

ANTHONY: He's the cynic here.

MADELEINE: I think it's a miracle.

ANTHONY: (*Bowing to MADELEINE.*) Thank you… Thank you…

ANTHONY exits into the kitchen. Silence. The crackle and hum of early evening sounds outside.

LUCIEN: Anthony says you –

MADELEINE: I'm just passing through. I work these places in the summer.

LUCIEN: And in the winter –

MADELEINE: I move on. Wherever. I like to keep on the move. Whatever brings the money in.

Silence.

LUCIEN: I don't want to think what he's doing in there –

MADELEINE: You work? I see you brought your work –

Silence. MADELEINE and LUCIEN look at one another.

LUCIEN: It's boring.

MADELEINE shrugs.

Risk assessment. I assess the risk to small companies. Mainly the young start-ups. I work out what they must look out for, the potential pitfalls professionally and financially.

MADELEINE looks at him. Silence.

It's boring. Desk bound. (*Beat.*) Do you always –

MADELEINE: What?

LUCIEN: …ask so many questions?

MADELEINE: I only asked the one.

Silence.

LUCIEN: He talks a lot. Some people find it difficult. He's always been a live wire. I don't mind it. You get used to it. It's what makes up him.

A crash from the kitchen. Silence. LUCIEN gets up to exit into the kitchen.

MADELEINE: Why do you let him tell that story –

LUCIEN stops midway.

…if you don't believe it?

LUCIEN: It's not that I don't believe it. It's just not freak. There's a logic. If you asses it, the logic. There's always a logic, you can always find logic for accidental events.

MADELEINE: I don't think that's true.

LUCIEN: We are all a kind of semi-conductor. The best place to stand with intense meteorological activity, namely lightning, is a wide open place. The safest place. By confining himself within the width of a metal porch, Anthony placed himself within a perfect circuit – Lightning. Letterbox. Chest. Kapow. The rubber acts as a simple circuit break.

MADELEINE: So where does that leave miracle? Miracles don't have logic, that's what makes them miracles.

Silence.

LUCIEN: We were six, we were only six years old.

MADELEINE: Miracles –

LUCIEN: No.

MADELEINE: …miracles can happen.

LUCIEN: No.

Silence.

MADELEINE: It's a good story.

LUCIEN: It's a good story. He likes telling it. I like hearing it. That's all that matters. (*Beat.*) You weren't there.

MADELEINE shrugs, smiles.

He lost someone. I'm kind to him. Someone he loved very much. I'm perhaps kind to him, kinder than I would be –

Another crash from the kitchen. LUCIEN turns, tenses –

MADELEINE: I got it wrong.

Silence.

I'm sorry.

LUCIEN stares at her. Too long.

LUCIEN: He's an accident waiting to happen.

MADELEINE wets the rim of her glass. A long low hum.

You look…you look like someone we used to know.

A crackle of electricity. ANTHONY enters.

Sense that the evening has moved on – More relaxed. Laughter. Scene springs back into life. A crackle of electricity. Sense that the evening has moved on further – More relaxed. Laughter. MADELEINE is mid drinking game. LUCIEN is clearly wilting –

ANTHONY: Hello Harry it is Harry…

MADELEINE: Then you've got to say who's Harry?

ANTHONY: He's too pissed. I tell you, I've never seen you so pissed.

LUCIEN: *Hello Harry. It's Harry.* I don't get this game.

MADELEINE: (*Laughing.*) It doesn't matter.

ANTHONY: *Hello Harry. It's Harry. Can you tell Harry, that Harry wants him?* (*Finishes several drinks with certain aplomb.*)

LUCIEN: I don't get it. I still don't get it.

MADELEINE insists on pouring them another round. A crackle of electricity. Sense that the evening has moved on further – More relaxed. Mellow. They're lying flat on their backs, as if staring up at the stars.

ANTHONY: *Fuck you, you mother fucker.*

MADELEINE: Where?

ANTHONY: (*Pointing up to the stars.*) If you join the three witches with that plough bit.

MADELEINE: I can't see it.

LUCIEN: He's dyslexic.

ANTHONY: (*Pointing up to the stars.*) *She's beautiful and we love her.*

MADELEINE: Where?

ANTHONY sits up, looking at MADELEINE.

I can't see it.

ANTHONY: Don't you think she is, Lucien?

MADELEINE: You two…you two are pulling my leg.

LUCIEN: We've drunk too much.

ANTHONY: You've drunk too much.

LUCIEN: Anthony, watch yourself, eh?

ANTHONY: Hear him? We've not drunk near enough.

A crackle of electricity. Sense that the evening has moved on further – Fun. Madness. ANTHONY suddenly pouncing on MADELEINE, a water bottle in his hand, sending shots of water, squirting out of his mouth.

MADELEINE: You've soaked me. You've soaked me.

MADELEINE sinks back down but is up again when – LUCIEN comes through also squirting water.

You're meant to be on my side. Jesus. Jesus.

MADELEINE gulps from her bottle of water and then she drenches both LUCIEN and ANTHONY who run, screaming away. A crackle of electricity. Sense that the evening has moved on further – Fun. More madness. A bee is buzzing around ANTHONY. He stands mouth open until – He closes his mouth. The buzzing grows silent.

MADELEINE: If it stings –

LUCIEN: Yes.

MADELEINE: If it stings, it will make your tongue swell.

LUCIEN: (*Beat.*) Anthony. (*Beat.*) Anthony, please.

A sense of suspended silence until – ANTHONY opens his mouth. The buzzing resumes and flies away.

ANTHONY: He hates it when I do that.

MADELEINE: It's magic.

LUCIEN: It's stupid.

ANTHONY: He's always like this.

LUCIEN: If you get stung –

MADELEINE: Do you put something on your tongue?

ANTHONY ruffles LUCIEN's hair.

ANTHONY: I didn't so we're fine.

LUCIEN: I'm just saying.

MADELEINE: (*To LUCIEN.*) Have another drink. Go on. You're on holiday.

LUCIEN holds up his glass.

ANTHONY: See, see she's good for us.

MADELEINE and LUCIEN are staring up at AN-THONY who is trying to climb the pylon.

LUCIEN: Get down you bloody nutter.

MADELEINE: Anthony, come down.

ANTHONY: I will now prove my theory. That man cannot fly unaided.

ANTHONY jumps and goes crashing to the ground, landing flat on the floor. LUCIEN and MADELEINE run to pick ANTHONY up. ANTHONY lies very still. A growing panic until ANTHONY sits up and plants kisses on both LUCIEN and MADELEINE.

My point indeed proved.

A crackle of electricity. Sense that the evening has moved on further – The early hours of the morning.

MADELEINE: And sometimes I think this will be the place. This will be the place. I stop. I stay.

A crackle of electricity. Sense that the evening has moved on further – Dawn. Mellow. A little dangerous. MADELEINE, LUCIEN and ANTHONY lie on their backs staring up at the early morning sunrise. Suddenly all the lights go out, distant music goes silent.

It's the cinema screen, they put up a cinema screen, it drains the electricity. You can be half way through cooking your dinner and that's it, stops for the night. Like there's not enough electricity, there's not enough power to go round then suddenly you get that surge. –

Silence.

(*Pointing to stars.*) Time for bed.

ANTHONY: (*Pointing to stars.*) Not yet.

Silence.

LUCIEN: (*Pointing to stars.*) Stay here if you want to.

MADELEINE stops, about to get up.

MADELEINE: Where does it say that?

ANTHONY: Yeah, where does it say that?

LUCIEN: Sorry. I thought it was a star. Aeroplane.

ANTHONY: That fucks up your whole sentence. (*Beat.*) Stay here if you want to.

Silence.

MADELEINE: *So who do I sleep with?*

Silence. MADELEINE laughs. LUCIEN and AN-THONY get up. They stand awkwardly.

Night.

MADELEINE exits, laughing.

ANTHONY: Night.

Silence. They linger.

(*To LUCIEN.*) Great girl.

LUCIEN: Great girl.

LUCIEN nods. He scoops up the glasses and heads inside.

Door?

ANTHONY: Lock.

LUCIEN: Progress.

The cross beam of headlights as MADELEINE hitches a lift home. ANTHONY stares as if watching her.

The Lake

MADELEINE lies on a pontoon, flat on her back, reading from a newspaper. LUCIEN dries himself post swim. ANTHONY lounges next to them, sunbathing.

MADELEINE: A woman was out to lunch with her husband celebrating their twenty-fifth wedding anniversary, delighted with the pearl necklace he had just given her. (*To LUCIEN and ANTHONY.*) Yeah right.

LUCIEN: What's funny about that?

ANTHONY: He's such an innocent.

MADELEINE: You don't know what a pearl necklace is?

ANTHONY: It's like giving a girl a golden shower, without the wee wee.

Silence.

LUCIEN: I still don't get it.

ANTHONY: (*To MADELEINE.*) Shall I go on with this?

MADELEINE: Protect him.

ANTHONY: Protect him.

LUCIEN: Tell me.

ANTHONY: Best not.

MADELEINE: However as the lunch progressed, it became clear that this was not a time of celebration, the husband asked his wife for a divorce. The man had fallen in love and planned to marry his very elegant female boss as soon as his rather frumpy wife agreed. A heated argument ensued spilling to outside the restaurant, the wife furious to learn of her husband's infidelity. In a moment's rage the wife clawed at the pearls around her neck, preparing to throw them back in his face. Pulling them with such a velocity, they fired like bullets through the air.

LUCIEN: God, I get it. That's disgusting. Is that what a pearl necklace is?

ANTHONY: It can be pleasurable.

LUCIEN: I don't want to know.

MADELEINE: A young man en route to work, and busy talking on the telephone to his therapist, was momentarily distracted by the site of a pearl flying across his eyeline. The young man walked into a tree and promptly snapped his neck.

The sound of trees, a branch snapping in the woods.

(*Turning to LUCIEN.*) It's kind of sick.

ANTHONY: It's his porn.

LUCIEN: It's not my porn.

ANTHONY: For the anal and insane. He likes to decode them. He gets bored. He gets bored, very easily.

LUCIEN: It's my job. Some of these are classic.

ANTHONY sinks back onto the pontoon.

Don't you see these are classic?

ANTHONY: Some bored tea boy with fuck all to do all day. (*Beat.*) His grammar's shite.

MADELEINE: The therapist continued talking for a full thirty-two seconds before noticing her client had grown silent. The husband recovered thirty-nine of the forty-seven dropped pearls. Eight are still not accounted for.

ANTHONY: Freaky. (*To MADELEINE.*) Watch and learn, this is how you argue –

LUCIEN: I'm not going to argue.

ANTHONY: (*To MADELEINE.*) You ready? Because it is coming.

MADELEINE: What?

ANTHONY: A full grown woman –

LUCIEN: Here we go again.

ANTHONY: …can't be killed by a sandwich.

LUCIEN: If she's standing –

ANTHONY: Even if she's standing –

LUCIEN: …in the wrong place at the right time. A sandwich could hit her. Trigger a heart attack.

ANTHONY: A penny maybe. A penny if dropped could kill you.

LUCIEN: Height plus velocity equals mass… Doesn't matter what size it is, if dropped from a large height, it gathers speed, passes through time, builds momentum, gathers mass and –

MADELEINE: A sandwich is tiny, a sandwich is a soft thing –

LUCIEN: Height plus velocity, it gathers momentum. The softest things can –

MADELEINE: A soft thing can't kill you.

LUCIEN: If dropped from the right height can have an effect. (*Beat.*)

ANTHONY: Okay, you could die but it's pretty fucking freaky. Passing at the exact moment –

LUCIEN: It's science, it's pure science. There's nothing freak about it.

MADELEINE: Being killed by a flying sandwich I think is pretty strange.

LUCIEN: It's the cause that means it's not freak, as long as there is a cause, one can always find the science for the effect. A man is unfaithful – cause. His wife rages breaking her necklace – effect. A pearl goes flying – cause, it distracts a man who breaks his neck – effect.

ANTHONY: A woman with a crooked nose –

Silence. LUCIEN does not stir.

A woman with a crooked nose and funny hair jumps from a bridge.

Silence.

LUCIEN: Which bridge?

Silence.

Height is important.

ANTHONY: (*Cutting in.*) It doesn't really matter.

MADELEINE: Was this in the paper?

ANTHONY: There's water underneath.

LUCIEN: I don't want to play this.

ANTHONY: Where's the cause? (*Beat.*) Where's the cause, Lucien?

Silence.

LUCIEN: The jump.

ANTHONY: That's the effect.

LUCIEN holds ANTHONY's gaze.

LUCIEN: She fell.

ANTHONY: Still has to be a cause. If there's no cause, I'd say that was a freak fucking accident.

LUCIEN: She didn't jump.

ANTHONY: If she jumped it's a fucking tragedy.

Silence.

MADELEINE: Is it in a back copy?

MADELEINE searches through the newspapers –

ANTHONY: No.

MADELEINE: It's an actual true story?

Silence. LUCIEN is clearly struggling. ANTHONY goes to touch him.

ANTHONY: It's a miracle.

MADELEINE: Where's the miracle?

LUCIEN: Yeah, Anthony, where's the miracle.

LUCIEN holds ANTHONY's look.

ANTHONY: The miracle is… She's still alive.

LUCIEN suddenly gets up, MADELEINE stops searching.

LUCIEN: I might have a swim.

ANTHONY: A boat. A boat sailing underneath breaks her fall. I might come with you.

LUCIEN: No, why don't you stay? Why don't you stay and talk to Madeleine?

ANTHONY stands as if to stop LUCIEN, wanting to reach out and touch him in some way.

I won't be a minute.

ANTHONY continues almost to bar LUCIEN's path.

Stay. I just want to swim. Okay?

LUCIEN swims off.

Silence.

MADELEINE: Is there something I'm missing?

Silence.

ANTHONY: Do you know the San Francisco' Golden Gate is not the biggest bridge?

ANTHONY watches LUCIEN swim away.

It's a bridge somewhere in China.

MADELEINE: I didn't know that.

ANTHONY: Yeah, people often make the mistake.

Silence.

The second's somewhere in Asia, one of the Arab states. They've got a lot of money. They can afford the bricks.

Silence.

MADELEINE: What just happened there?

ANTHONY: Lucien? That's just Lucien. He doesn't talk about stuff.

MADELEINE: Not talking –

ANTHONY: That's what I tell him –

MADELEINE: Not talking is bad for you.

Silence.

Do you do this, do you two come away together like this a lot?

ANTHONY shrugs, still looking out for LUCIEN.

ANTHONY: This holiday. This little trip. It's part of a routine. He picks me up, he cleans me up, gets my hair cut, buys me new clothes. I tell him. I say – *I don't care what I wear.* He gives me money. He tells me not to spend it too quick. I say – *I won't.* I always do. I don't mean to let him down. I think he feels I let him down. Last time he found me licking the pavement. He thinks I've lost hope. I just like the taste.

ANTHONY sees MADELEINE looking at him.

We get through it. Normally. He feels better. I look good as new. (*Silence.*) Don't be sorry for me.

ANTHONY looks out as if searching for LUCIEN.

The funniest thing is I'm happy. I don't think I've ever been happier in my life.

Silence.

MADELEINE: She's someone you knew.

ANTHONY holds her look. MADELEINE goes to touch him.

Can I do something? Is there anything I can do to help?

Static. She pulls her hand back –

ANTHONY: I don't know yet. I'm not sure yet. Miracles don't work like that.

Suddenly from under the pontoon, LUCIEN bursts up out of the water, gasping for breath.

LUCIEN: Did you see me? Wow, did you see me?

MADELEINE keeps staring at ANTHONY.

ANTHONY: (*Beat.*) No. You vanished.

MADELEINE keeps staring at ANTHONY.

You completely disappeared.

The Deck

ANTHONY sitting in the last of the sun, oblivious to bees buzzing around him, reading the newspaper. LUCIEN sits working.

The crackle of the electricity pylon above.

ANTHONY: A farmer and his younger brother decided to remove a bees' nest from a shed on their property with the aid of a pineapple, an illegal firework more appropriately used for large displays, with the explosive equivalent of one half stick of dynamite. They light the fuse and retreat to watch from a window inside their home ten feet away from the hive-stroke-shed. The ricochet of the explosion though successfully destroying the bees nest, shatters the glass, leaving the brother with slight grazes which the farmer decides need medical attention at once. Whilst waiting for the brother in casualty, the farmer is hungry and decides to walk to the local fruit store. Choosing a peach from a large display in the shop window, he purchases and walks back in the midday sun. The farmer takes a bite of his peach en route. A lazy bee is dozing on its skin. The farmer is stung three times by the insect and immediately collapses. An ambulance is called. Unbeknownst to either the farmer or the brother, both are allergic to the venom of the bee. In casualty for the second time that day the farmer dies. The brother, in mourning, asks for the gloves that the farmer once wore. The brother goes home to tell his wife of the farmer's death, unaware that a bee, still alive, is sleeping in the finger of the glove. Bracing himself to go in and tell the news of the farmer's death, the brother slips on the gloves as a tribute to times gone.

ANTHONY pauses, he slowly starts to rip the page. LUCIEN tries to ignore him.

Fortunately the glove has a small hole in the index finger, a hole that he was sure had never been there before. The bee flies away just as the brother is slipping on the glove. The brother is amazed and sees life anew. He begins to throw parties, he invites in the neighbours, gives them free steaks for life and rogers his wife for the first time in ages, a woman who had forgotten what a good shag was.

A long low drone of car horns in the distance, making ANTHONY jump, turn suddenly as –

LUCIEN: They're too noisy with their cars.

ANTHONY: People are celebrating. It's summer, people do that.

LUCIEN: You don't drive. Cars are for driving, not public holidays.

ANTHONY: I'm glad I don't drive.

LUCIEN: You used to.

ANTHONY: Exactly.

LUCIEN: It makes a life a lot easier. You can always get away.

ANTHONY: You never leave the city.

LUCIEN: You always say this.

ANTHONY: ...a few weeks in the summer? Yeah, right, Luce, let your hair down.

LUCIEN: If you drove I wouldn't have to do everything.

ANTHONY: Like what?

LUCIEN: Like the shopping?

ANTHONY: You get it delivered.

LUCIEN: I'm just saying.

ANTHONY: Why?

LUCIEN: It means I have to do it all.

LUCIEN returns to his work. He clocks the box of vegetables.

Did Madeleine –

ANTHONY: (*Shakes head.*) Bloke, her day off. She's great isn't she?

LUCIEN: Who?

ANTHONY: Madeleine.

LUCIEN: You fall in love with –

ANTHONY: No.

LUCIEN: …women on adverts. Women we passed on the way here.

ANTHONY: No. She's –

LUCIEN: Very attractive. You want to fuck her?

ANTHONY: No. (*Beat.*) Yes but –

LUCIEN: You want to fuck her.

ANTHONY: I don't see…I really don't see anything wrong in that.

LUCIEN: You wouldn't.

ANTHONY: What you getting at?

Silence.

What you getting at?

Silence.

MADELEINE passes placing a punnet of strawberries in LUCIEN's hands. He looks up, oblivious.

LUCIEN: Did you order strawberries?

ANTHONY shakes his head. The distant toot of horns, a celebration far off –

ANTHONY: I was thinking. I was thinking I might go out tonight.

The crackle of the electricity above moving into a long low hum.

The Wood

The glow of a cinema screen down on –

LUCIEN, ANTHONY and MADELEINE sitting looking up. ANTHONY keeps standing up, wanting to move closer to the screen.

LUCIEN: Quit doing that –

ANTHONY: The quality –

LUCIEN: …the people behind can't see.

ANTHONY: …is fucking abysmal.

LUCIEN: He's an authority.

> *MADELEINE laughs.*

He is now an authority on the cinema screen.

MADELEINE: They hire it locally. It's normally for Karaoke.

LUCIEN: We're not in the city.

ANTHONY: (*Shouting.*) Everyone has heard of DVD?

> *Silence. The muffled soundtrack. ANTHONY stands up again.*

LUCIEN: You're making it impossible –

ANTHONY: It's impossible to see.

LUCIEN: It's meant to be a bit blurry. It's underwater.

ANTHONY: This film is ancient.

MADELEINE: Anthony sit down. I'm enjoying it.

ANTHONY: (*Sits down.*) Sorry. Okay. Fine.

Silence. The muffle of the soundtrack.

(*To MADELEINE.*) But I am right aren't I?

MADELEINE tries not to laugh.

LUCIEN: Anthony –

ANTHONY: Sorry, okay. Sorry.

Silence. The muffle of the soundtrack.

(*Beat.*) I think it's absolutely wonderful. This film is an absolute delight.

LUCIEN: I'm going to hammer you.

ANTHONY: (*To MADELEINE.*) This is the moment I've been waiting for.

LUCIEN: Are you going to shut up? You're being a fucking arse now. People are getting pissed off.

They fight.

MADELEINE: Will you two cut it out?

They stop fighting.

Silence. The muffle of the soundtrack.

ANTHONY lets out a long fart.

They fight.

How old are you two? Will you stop it?

LUCIEN concedes, but ANTHONY is still going. He starts dancing, performing, acting out the movie, it's moving from funny to verging on the weird.

Anthony…Anthony. What you doing what you doing?

LUCIEN: Anthony.

ANTHONY stops. Silence. LUCIEN sinks back to watching the film.

ANTHONY: What?

LUCIEN: You just always take it too far.

ANTHONY: Nobody asked you to come.

ANTHONY sinks back down. MADELEINE shifts to make room for him.

Jesus. Who asked you, eh?

LUCIEN's gaze flicks to MADELEINE, ANTHONY clocks this, realises –

Silence.

ANTHONY leans over and punches LUCIEN in the arm; hard. LUCIEN flinches but doesn't take his eyes off from watching the cinema screen.

Silence.

LUCIEN: I'll get us something to drink.

A long low hum, crickets, sounds of the night through –

A Roadstop

LUCIEN is standing, having just bought bottles of beer. He turns and sees MADELEINE standing, facing him. The beam of car headlights, as cars go past.

MADELEINE: I thought you might need a hand –

LUCIEN shrugs –

It's nearly the intermission.

MADELEINE takes her beer. They stand and drink.

LUCIEN: He's sometimes weird like that. People don't always get him. He's harmless. But I can see he could be frightening.

MADELEINE: No.

LUCIEN: Good.

Silence.

MADELEINE: You don't talk much.

LUCIEN: Enough. (*Beat.*) Has Anthony said something. You've probably noticed... He likes you. He doesn't mean to be an idiot. Be careful with him.

MADELEINE: He's not going to break. (*Silence.*) He's a grown man.

LUCIEN: Hardly. Sometimes he frightens people.

MADELEINE: I'm not frightened.

LUCIEN: Good...good...

LUCIEN makes to go.

MADELEINE: Lucien –

LUCIEN stops –

I had a dream last night –

The steady cross beam of passing headlights.

LUCIEN: Yeah?

MADELEINE: Yeah. (*Beat.*) You were in it. You and Anthony. I think we'd been drinking. We were drinking but no I wasn't, I didn't feel, I didn't feel drunk.

LUCIEN: Teetotal dreams. They never work.

MADELEINE half laughs. Silence.

MADELEINE: It's dark, night. I'm walking up this road, it's really busy. Cars are dodging me, it's like they're weaving to miss me –

LUCIEN: They would.

MADELEINE: Yeah… It's this blur of red and white, back and forth. I've no shoes on, I'm laughing – I don't know why I find it so funny. Cars are swaying, like drunks in the road. I feel really cold.

LUCIEN: You don't feel temperature, you can't really feel temperature in your dream.

MADELEINE: I wasn't wearing anything. I don't wear anything in bed –

Silence.

LUCIEN: Right. (*Silence.*) It would be it.

MADELEINE: I was cold. I'm on a bridge. It's a bridge, any moment now, there'll be a flying sandwich eh?

LUCIEN: Yeah.

MADELEINE: And that's when I turn and see you. Looking at me. And I'm not laughing. I'm crying. I wake up and I'm crying. You said something to me. In my dream that – when I wake up I'm crying. I don't know what you say but – I think I jumped. I think I jumped.

LUCIEN puts out his hand as if almost to catch her. She looks at him as he holds both her arms.

The sound of the intermission music kicking in far off –

It's not me who's frightened is it? (*Silence.*) Is it?

Silence.

The Lake

Darkness. Laughter far off. The glow of a cinema screen across the lake. ANTHONY and LUCIEN stand dripping wet. Distant sound of MADELEINE jumping. ANTHONY and LUCIEN both watch in suspended silence until MADELEINE comes up. They cheer and clap. She enters dripping.

ANTHONY: Your turn.

LUCIEN: I'm not good at –

ANTHONY pushes him. Sound of LUCIEN falling, suspended silence until –

Sound of LUCIEN coming up.

MADELEINE: (*Calling out.*) You have to swim the whole length.

ANTHONY: (*Calling out.*) The whole length. We're watching you.

Silence. MADELEINE and ANTHONY slump down on the ground.

He's too slow. I like it here.

MADELEINE: I get restless. It's the darkness, the stillness.

They listen.

It's fine in the summer but – Soon they'll have the highest rainfall this side of – Whatever. It gets wet. Summer over. You don't want to get used to it. Get used to it. Then see how you feel. If I get used to it, then I die.

ANTHONY: Drama queen.

They listen.

I like it. I quite like it.

They listen.

There's wild cats. It's never still with wildcats moving around.

MADELEINE: Who told you that?

ANTHONY: Lucien said –

MADELEINE: Cats… There are probably a few cats in the wood. And foxes eating from the bins, getting into people's houses.

Dots of lights above them. ANTHONY bends low.

Fireflies.

ANTHONY and MADELEINE watch as they skim the water. ANTHONY nods.

ANTHONY: Fireflies.

They watch the lake. Distant sounds of the cinema, water, trees.

MADELEINE: Where would you like to be?

ANTHONY: Now?

MADELEINE: In five years' time.

A firefly skims close. MADELEINE moves as if watching it.

ANTHONY: I don't think about that. Wherever.

MADELEINE: Somewhere. It has to be somewhere.

Silence.

ANTHONY: I'd like to love someone. I'd like to love someone I guess. I'd like to be living – I don't know if it will be a house. Maybe somewhere on the…South

China sea. We might have children. I'll probably have a job by then.

MADELEINE: With a suit.

ANTHONY: Not a suit.

Silence.

Flip flops and a snorkel.

Silence.

And I'll be… I'll be better by then

A second firefly skims close.

Jesus did you see that one?

MADELEINE keeps watching him. Fireflies gradually start to land on him through the following –

MADELEINE: And where will Lucien be?

ANTHONY: In a tiny box, very high up, screwing his secretary.

MADELEINE: I hope not.

ANTHONY: With a weight problem and a hernia, somewhere painful, from all the stress.

Silence.

MADELEINE: Maybe I should take your seat back.

Silence.

ANTHONY: Sure. I'll deliver vegetables. That sounds great. I'd like that. Only Lucien wouldn't let me go.

Silence.

MADELEINE: You sure it's not the other way around?

Silence.

Does Lucien have someone, does Lucien have anyone back home?

Silence.

ANTHONY: In the city?

MADELEINE nods.

Lucien. No. No. No one would have him.

Silence.

He lost someone.

MADELEINE: He did?

ANTHONY: He thinks I don't appreciate. I do. I do. I know how much she meant to him.

Silence.

You know he has this flat, where everything is very neat?

MADELEINE: You're glowing.

ANTHONY: He's anal. He's really very anal.

ANTHONY is slowly glowing brighter through the following.

He's window boxes, and books, and a really too comfy sofa. He comes home every night on time. He has pictures on his wall. He has toilet cleaner and a loo brush.

MADELEINE: Anthony –

ANTHONY: Sometimes when he's found me I've cacked in my pants. I've been living off liquid. I'm lying in the gutter.

Silence.

I'm fine. I'm doing fine.

In the distance, LUCIEN calling –

He's the one I worry about.

LUCIEN calling, closer now.

LUCIEN: (*Calling out.*) Here I come.

MADELEINE stands astonished, as ANTHONY stands aglow with fireflies. He reaches out to touch her as –

ANTHONY: I'm only telling you –

As LUCIEN heaves himself up on the deck, pausing on seeing.

He's the weirdo.

ANTHONY his head glowing then suddenly – LUCIEN watches amazed as one last firefly hovers around ANTHONY's head. ANTHONY holds LUCIEN's gaze.

The House

A beam of headlights, across LUCIEN. He is alone.

LUCIEN: A woman – (*Beat.*) …a woman with a crooked nose – (*Beat.*) …a woman with a crooked nose and a voice, a low, gasping voice met her friends on a bridge for a day out; two boys, now men, she had known for years. The three friends, the three points of the same triangle, spent the day together reminiscing over times gone by and a friendship which had weathered most things in their relatively short lives. The two men laughed at her life, unsuspecting that she had a surprise for them. Returning to the bridge that evening, the woman informed them that she intended to take her life. The woman, who was not drunk at the time and who had in fact matched her friends' many alcoholic beverages with the clarity of water, knew her mind. Stepping into the road, she weaved her way in amongst the speeding traffic, ignoring the childish laughter and drunken grasps of her two friends, who should have known better. (*Beat.*) Should have known. (*Beat.*) Standing with her arms out, ready to take the approaching juggernaut, the two friends were quickly sobered to the idea that this was indeed a woman of her word. They pulled her out of the way. Congratulating themselves as heroes what the two failed to recognise was that the woman was more determined that they thought. Climbing over the railings of the metal bridge, the quieter of the two, the shy boy moved forward to stop her and it was then that she asked the fateful question – *Who loves me? Who loves me the most?* The shy boy knew what was in his heart and that is what she needed to hear. But he also knew the truth would hurt the runt boy – Kapow – kapow. She fell… She fell.

The slam of the door – ANTHONY comes out, his wet costume in his hand which he slings on the side.

ANTHONY: Wild cats got into your beer.

LUCIEN scoops up the wet costume, going to hang it up –

LUCIEN: (*Beat.*) You're drinking too much again.

ANTHONY: Finished the rest of the cornflakes too. You think they'd have more sophisticated tastes.

LUCIEN: Why were you weird tonight?

ANTHONY: She didn't mind –

LUCIEN: You want your towel hung out?

ANTHONY: How old am I, Lucien? (*Beat.*) Don't treat me like I'm ten.

Silence.

LUCIEN: I'm trying to help you. I'm trying to help you get yourself cleaned up.

ANTHONY: What's wrong with being dirty, Luce? What's wrong with me?

Silence.

LUCIEN: You sleep in the gutter.

ANTHONY: I like it. It's the way I feel. I'm living the life the way I feel.

LUCIEN: Something could happen to you. It's dangerous.

ANTHONY: More dangerous than the way you live your life? Keys. Door. Progress. When was the last time you had sex, Lucien?

Silence.

Mine was stood up behind a bar, with some woman I'd met that morning. It was nice. We were drunk. It was something.

LUCIEN: It's fucking sordid.

LUCIEN makes to go in.

ANTHONY: It's living. It's living with it Lucien.

Silence.

Luce –

LUCIEN: Don't be fucked off with me, because you didn't get a shag.

Silence.

ANTHONY: I'm working on it.

LUCIEN: You're only here for the summer.

ANTHONY: So?

LUCIEN: She's a nice girl.

ANTHONY: So?

LUCIEN: You think you can give her a good time? Take her out to nice places?

ANTHONY: Yeah.

LUCIEN: It'll be me paying for it.

ANTHONY: I'm not stopping you.

Silence.

Everyman for himself eh?

Silence.

Christ, it's called taking a risk, Luce.

Silence. A bee buzzes around LUCIEN.

LUCIEN: Risk. What risk do you take? A bee, you catch a bee in your hand, you hold it in your hand and you expect us all to be impressed. When have you ever been stung?

A bee buzzes around LUCIEN.

Never. No danger.

LUCIEN lets it land on his hand. He tentatively clasps it until –

It's called understanding risk.

Suddenly LUCIEN pulls back his hand, stung.

Every time.

LUCIEN sucks on his hand. ANTHONY goes to help him. LUCIEN pulls away.

ANTHONY: Maybe I just don't tell you if I have.

LUCIEN: You? You couldn't keep your mouth shut –

ANTHONY: No.

LUCIEN: Yes.

Silence.

Being crazy is easy.

LUCIEN makes to go inside.

ANTHONY: I want to fit, Lucien. I want to be normal. I just don't know how to be. I don't want to be like this. I want to be quiet, still. I want to not bother you. I want to get my own hair cut. I want to go to sleep not thinking about *her*. Luce – If I could fit. I would. I would try and fit. I would put my money in a bank. I would walk on the pavement. I wouldn't crawl. But this is what I am, this is it, Lucien. It would take a miracle –

LUCIEN wavers, wants to touch him.

LUCIEN: Don't leave that stuff on the line all night.

LUCIEN exits. ANTHONY sits on his own. Suddenly, he reaches up and grasps the light bulb above

him, holding it tight, burning himself until – It breaks
in his hand, blood.

The Wood

The glow of a cinema screen down on – ANTHONY sitting
as if watching.

ANTHONY: There was this old blind lady and she lived,
  I think it was Miami – you know, one of those places
  with a pool, where everyone else is old, and there's lots
  of palm trees and those little buggies that you wheel
  around in if you're playing golf. Her family had farmed
  her out there, she'd grown up in Vancouver. She liked
  seasons and changes but in Miami it was always hot.
  Every year her family would call her, just before Christmas, saying they'd come down and fly her back for the
  weekend so she could feel the snow, or a cold wind,
  just what she missed living always with palm trees –
  every year they would make this promise.
  'See you soon, Grandma.'
  She'd wait, and she'd wait but they never would turn
  up. Her grandson was called…it doesn't matter what
  he was called but he was her favourite, he was her best
  boy. He'd always send a Christmas card.
  'Sorry I can't make it.'
  There was a mail guy who delivered letters to the old
  blind lady every day and after a while he realised that
  she was waiting for a letter that would never come,
  a visitor who would never arrive, a special day that
  would never happen. He felt sorry for her. He liked
  her. He always made sure he said 'hello' – just chit-chat,
  nothing much – just the time of day.
  Christmas came, it got hotter. The mail guy decided to
  clean up his flat. A small place – one room. It wasn't
  as if anyone was going to call. He didn't have many

friends. He lived mainly on take-away and those instant meals you heat up. No-one even missed him. His neighbours could never remember his name. It was then he found the letter, a Christmas card to the old lady, lost in the seam of his mail bag, released when shaken out.

A Christmas card, glitter, he could feel it through the envelope, a picture of mountains: Vancouver, somewhere like that. He would visit her, deliver it. His job was important to him. And it wasn't as if he had anything else to do. He knocked on her door.

'Berni.' The grandson was called Berni. 'Berni, is that you, darling?'

'Mrs Adams, I've got a card for you – '

'Berni, will you come in now?'

She looked him straight in the face. There were flowers on the table and a turkey slowly roasting. She had a record on, any old record, the house felt different.

'Where are you?' The old lady cried, feeling his face.

'I'm here,' said the mail guy.

'Sit down, Berni.'

So he sat down, and they ate together, pulling crackers and he took her for a drive in his mail car and he took her to the cooling fridge at the postal plant where they kept all the cold mail, turkeys and stuff that people have sent for Christmas.

'This is cooler than Vancouver, Berni.'

'It is Grandma. It's even got snow, feel?'

And they danced to her record and he thanked her for the socks. And when he said goodbye, she said:

'Don't be a stranger now,' in a way that made the mail guy want to cry. This was the first Christmas in years he'd not been alone.

'Same time next year.'

'Same time next year,' said the mail guy. As he was going the old blind lady said:

'You've dropped your card, Berni,' picking it up on the mantelpiece, where it was left.
'It's for you,' said the mail guy.
'I don't need it.'
Miracle. It would take a miracle.

The flicker of a cinema screen. Surge of music. ANTHO-NY shoves a large handful of popcorn in his mouth –

The Deck

Day; MADELEINE stands with a picnic basket. ANTHONY stands brushing his teeth. LUCIEN reads the morning paper, drinking coffee. It is raining.

MADELEINE: So I was thinking –

LUCIEN: I've a lot of work to do.

MADELEINE: You take a boat, they're just a group of caves, but they're beautiful. Everyone goes…everyone goes at this time of year.

ANTHONY: Sounds great. (*Silence.*) You brought food?

MADELEINE: Leftovers from the restaurant.

ANTHONY: We eat leftovers.

MADELEINE: I was thinking after –

ANTHONY snatches LUCIEN's newspaper off him.

I could cook you dinner here.

ANTHONY: That would be great. (*To LUCIEN.*) Wouldn't that be great?

LUCIEN: We've nothing in.

ANTHONY: We can pick up stuff. (*To MADELEINE.*) Thank you.

Silence.

LUCIEN: How far away is it?

MADELEINE: It's near. It's near the lake.

ANTHONY: Where's your sense of adventure? He'd love to come. We'd both love to come.

MADELEINE looks to LUCIEN.

That's just the way his face falls.

A Cave

MADELEINE, ANTHONY and LUCIEN standing in a boat in the cave.

ANTHONY: (*Calling out.*) Madeleine.

MADELEINE: (*Calling out.*) Anthony.

ANTHONY: (*Calling out.*) Lucien. (*Silence.*) No echo.

LUCIEN: It swallows you.

Silence.

MADELEINE: The sound, the sound escapes, see, see the light?

LUCIEN and ANTHONY look up.

LUCIEN: It's amazing.

ANTHONY: It's an escape route.

MADELEINE: Where to?

ANTHONY: Anywhere you want to.

Silence.

Why don't you have my seat back to the city?

LUCIEN laughs.

LUCIEN: Don't be daft.

ANTHONY: I'm serious. I've been thinking. It's quieter here. The people are nicer. They'll need someone to take that cinema screen down in a couple of weeks. Tourists leave a mess. I could get a job clearing up.

LUCIEN: You get a job?

ANTHONY: Yeah. Maybe. It has happened before.

LUCIEN: You wouldn't do a thing here.

ANTHONY: Sometimes Lucien, your faith in me –

LUCIEN: You'd float on your back for weeks –

ANTHONY: Your faith in me is touching.

Silence.

(*Calling out.*) Touching.

Silence.

I'm hungry.

Silence. LUCIEN won't look at him.

It was only an idea.

A crackle of electricity; ripple of water. Sense of time moving on. Of them finishing off a picnic, sheltering by the side of –

The Lake

MADELEINE, LUCIEN and ANTHONY looking up at the rain clouds.

ANTHONY: (*Pointing to clouds.*) Hitler. With not much of a moustache.

LUCIEN: Hitler's not Hitler without his moustache.

ANTHONY: Turning into –

MADELEINE: Roger Rabbit.

ANTHONY: That's right, always go for the bunny.

LUCIEN: Your mum.

ANTHONY: With a hump? You're saying my mother had a hump?

MADELEINE: Does anybody want any more food?

ANTHONY: Stuffed.

LUCIEN: Ditto.

They sit in silence.

MADELEINE: Do you want to –

LUCIEN: No.

ANTHONY: I will.

LUCIEN: We should maybe get back soon.

ANTHONY: Too early.

MADELEINE: Way too early.

Silence. Awkward.

Okay, okay. We'll swim.

Silence. Awkward. The crackle of electricity, a ripple of water; a sense of time moving on to –

The Lake

The splash of water, as MADELEINE comes up from under the pontoon.

Drops of rain. Creak of trees.

LUCIEN sits under a rain coat.

Silence.

MADELEINE slides up next to him. He reads. She looks over his shoulder.

MADELEINE: Why you reading?

> *LUCIEN continues reading.*

LUCIEN: Don't know.

MADELEINE: It's upside down.

> *LUCIEN throws his book high into the water.*
>
> *MADELEINE laughs incredulous.*
>
> *LUCIEN laughs.*
>
> *Silence.*

MADELEINE: You should have a swim, concede defeat. It feels warm.

LUCIEN: Fucking fucking rain.

> *Silence.*

MADELEINE: Why do you tell Anthony there are wild cats? (*Silence.*) He's a grown man.

LUCIEN: He'd get lost.

MADELEINE: You'd find him.

LUCIEN: It's not the point to find him. It's the damage he does along the way.

MADELEINE: To who?

ANTHONY pulls himself up next to MADELEINE, bemused, catching their laughter.

Silence. They sit.

What do you hear?

ANTHONY: Birds. Trees creaking.

MADELEINE: Wild cats?

MADELEINE catches LUCIEN's eye.

ANTHONY: Sometimes. Maybe sometimes.

Trees cracking, sounds of the woods.

LUCIEN: They sound like voices.

MADELEINE: Sometimes.

LUCIEN: Like bits of conversations. Sometimes like whole bits of sentences.

ANTHONY: I can't hear them. What do they say?

Silence.

MADELEINE: It's cold.

ANTHONY and LUCIEN nod.

We should –

ANTHONY: Yeah.

LUCIEN: Yeah.

MADELEINE: Somewhere dry.

ANTHONY: Yeah.

LUCIEN: Yeah.

MADELEINE: Is this okay? (*Long silence.*) Say something. (*Silence.*) You know since I met you two I've never been so happy and never been so lonely in all my life. I don't know what it is but sometimes it's like – You remind me I'm on my own. And suddenly I don't like it. Suddenly it's not familiar. And I don't know where to go. I don't know where to go next.

The crackle of electricity, a ripple of water; a sense of time moving on to –

The House

Late; ANTHONY, LUCIEN and MADELEINE sitting in the dark. ANTHONY comes through with a bottle of whisky.

ANTHONY: Okay, okay. A middle-aged dentist was deeply in love with his beautiful fiancée. His only concern was the state of her teeth. As a man who came from a long line of dentists, he knew his mother would be critical of his bride. So he decides to give her a pre-nuptial agreement. High technology latex braces. Sort out her teeth in a sec. Driving her home to meet his mother for the first time, his fiancée decided to give her love a little present of her own. Midway through performing an act of, let's say, oral satisfaction, a small clip from her brace caught around the metal of his flies. The girl starts to choke as the dentist tried to unhook her. Unfortunately the guy was still driving at the time.

The car crashed. Kapow! They were both found dead in the wreckage.

MADELEINE: Punchline, punchline. You've got to have a punchline.

ANTHONY: The small latex brace was found hanging from the dead man's crotch.

LUCIEN: That's pathetic.

ANTHONY: With his fiancée's two front teeth still attached.

LUCIEN: Really lame.

ANTHONY pours them a whisky, LUCIEN shakes his head.

Silence.

They're only stories, Anthony.

ANTHONY: If they're only stories, Luce. I'll tell them how I want.

Silence.

A woman. A woman with a crooked nose and funny hair…

MADELEINE: I don't think we should do this.

ANTHONY: …a woman with a crooked nose and funny hair jumps from a bridge.

LUCIEN: I should drive you…I'll drive you home…

MADELEINE: You've drunk too much.

ANTHONY: The woman, a good friend –

LUCIEN: It's fine. You don't need to. We know how it ends.

ANTHONY: – the love of their life had spent the day reminiscing over times gone by and a friendship which had weathered most things in their relatively short lives. The two men laughed at her life, unsuspecting that she had a surprise for them. Returning to the bridge that evening, the woman informed them that she intended to take her life.

LUCIEN: She was drunk.

ANTHONY: She drank water all night.

LUCIEN: I don't want to do this now.

ANTHONY: The woman was someone who knew her own mind. The friends laughed. They didn't believe her.

LUCIEN: Why are you doing this?

ANTHONY: Standing with her arms out, ready to take the approaching juggernaut –

LUCIEN: Anthony please. Let's go home, we're going home soon.

ANTHONY: The two friends were quickly sobered to the idea that this was indeed a woman of her word. For what the woman wanted to know was – *Who loves me? Who loves me the most?* (*Silence.*) There's no such thing as a freak fucking accident. It's cause and effect, Luce. I know the effect. The one friend, a shy boy, was more sober than his drunk friend, he moved a little closer, he offered her words – *Who loves me? Who loves me the most?* You must have said something –

LUCIEN: The wind. The wind carried away my words.

ANTHONY: Who did you say? Luce, I know you said someone –

ANTHONY picks up the chairs and hurls it across the room. An angry, violent outburst, chairs, clothes, beer bottles go flying until –

LUCIEN: *Anthony.* I said…*Anthony…*

LUCIEN breaks down, pained, crumbling.

Silence. MADELEINE goes to touch LUCIEN, he withdraws.

Silence. ANTHONY watches.

ANTHONY: You stupid fuck.

The creak of trees. Rain.

You stupid, stupid fuck!

Silence.

You just had to say *Lucien.*

LUCIEN: We're going home.

ANTHONY: What do you hear, Lucien?

LUCIEN: I don't want to do this.

ANTHONY: You say you hear voices.

LUCIEN: I hear nothing.

ANTHONY: You hear something. It's not difficult. Close your eyes. Hear something. For Christ's sake, hear something! I can't do this all on my own. You stupid fuck. It didn't take much. It really didn't take much. You just had to say it. Luce, please. Tell me what you hear, please.

LUCIEN: 'You two – you two are terrible. But you love us. I love you.'

MADELEINE slowly kisses LUCIEN, first his hands, his back, his face as LUCIEN breaks down. ANTHONY watches; it is almost unbearable.

'I miss you…I love you… Both… You love us both… What's happened to Anthony's hair? It needs a cut. Make sure he gets a cut. You really aren't looking after him. Can't you look after him… Luce…Luce… You never looked after me.'

ANTHONY goes to touch LUCIEN, to try to quieten him but something makes him stop –

'Yes, you say you both love me, but look at you…'

MADELEINE and LUCIEN start to kiss, falling into making love.

MADELEINE: (*Whispered.*) Ssh –

ANTHONY exits.

Ssh –

The creak of the trees.

The Deck

The rain falls heavier as – A sudden surge of music, lights, every electrical gadget in the house whirring until –

ANTHONY wrapped with every wire and light in the house, a glowing, glittering raging ball, arms outstretched in the rain as if defying lightning to strike.

A power failure, all cuts out –

The House

Dawn; LUCIEN, MADELEINE and ANTHONY sit, exhausted, dripping wet. The house is chaos, chairs, tables everywhere.

Silence but for the drip of rain after the storm.

ANTHONY: A woman, once a girl, now a woman with –

LUCIEN: …a crooked nose.

ANTHONY: …with a crooked nose and hair –

LUCIEN: …funny hair –

ANTHONY: …with a crooked nose and funny hair…like a chicken met her friends on a bridge for a day out.

LUCIEN: Two boys, now men, she had known for years. Runt boy and shy boy, she'd given them these names. The three friends, the three points of the same triangle –

ANTHONY: …spent the day together reminiscing over times gone by and a friendship which had weathered most things in their relatively short lives.

LUCIEN: Returning to the bridge that evening, the woman informed them that she intended to take her life.

ANTHONY: Runt boy and shy boy knew they both loved her but at the moment when she should have known this.

LUCIEN: Kapow –

ANTHONY: Kapow – She jumped anyway.

Silence. MADELEINE puts the house in order throughout. Beat.

MADELEINE: However…

Silence. Both turn to look at MADELEINE.

ANTHONY: However – A boat carrying a cargo to –

LUCIEN: China.

ANTHONY: …China? A boat carrying a cargo of the finest flour –

LUCIEN: For dim sum.

ANTHONY: …for dim sum, was sailing underneath, when the captain, Captain –

MADELEINE: Captain Li –

ANTHONY: Okay, Captain Li – was looking up trying to navigate when he saw a young woman falling from the sky. The Captain, who was a clever man –

LUCIEN: And a world expert in calligraphy.

ANTHONY: Calligraphy? Calligraphy – He was a world expert in – anyway. Always useful. Captain Li, at the exact moment when he saw the young woman falling, pulled his boat up just in time for her –

LUCIEN: To land in the flour?

ANTHONY: To land in a mound of flour that left her completely white.

MADELEINE slowly starts to pick up the chairs, and tables, scooping up bottles around them, bringing order out of chaos.

LUCIEN: Captain Li – He had friends

ANTHONY: …who had a summer house off the South China sea –

Through the following, LUCIEN and ANTHONY watch MADELEINE as she tidies up around them.

LUCIEN: A yellow sea… Yellow from the sun and the fish that glinted in it. The Captain had friends, good friends, who heard the amazing story of the girl who jumped –

ANTHONY: And had a miraculous escape into the arms of Captain Li –

LUCIEN: They became lovers –

ANTHONY: They became lovers.

LUCIEN: And had several children. All called Confucius.

MADELEINE: It is believed that she is learning how to dive between China and the Bay of Bengal.

LUCIEN: Captain Li says that she's okay, that she's happy that – She's found a kind of happiness.

LUCIEN watches as a vase of flowers seems to float in front of him. MADELEINE places it on the table.

ANTHONY: *Who loves me? Who loves me the most?*

The sway of the trees outside, a distant creaking.

LUCIEN: Lucien.

ANTHONY puts his hand up. LUCIEN grips it, as if catching it, pulling him up stopping on seeing – A scorch mark, clear on the front of ANTHONY's shirt. MADELEINE goes to touch it.

ANTHONY: Kapow.

ANTHONY puts two fingers like a gun and shoots between his, LUCIEN and MADELEINE's heart.

Kapow. Kapow.

A long low hum, like the crackle of electricity, vibrating above as the lights go back on.

A Roadstop

LUCIEN is sitting in the car.

MADELEINE comes running out, with two coffees. She slides in next to him. They sit and drink.

LUCIEN: A rogue fork of lightning caught him hard across the chest. The boy fell down to the ground. He was only six years old.

Cars pass –

In years to come it was said that the boy possessed magic powers. In the darkest hour rumour had it that he shone.

They drive.

A Lake

ANTHONY swimming. The glow of fireflies.

A Motel

LUCIEN sits bolt upright, a sandwich comes flying down from above. LUCIEN catches it. He turns to see – the girl asleep next to him. LUCIEN contemplates. He eats the sandwich.

A car passes, its headlights beam across the stage.

The End.